Cornerstones of Freedom

The Jamestown Colony

Gail Sakurai

CHILDREN'S PRESS®
A Division of Grolier Publishing
New York • London • Hong Kong • Sydney
Danbury, Connecticut

Library of Congress Cataloging-in-Publication Data

Sakurai, Gail.
The Jamestown colony / Gail Sakurai.
    p. cm.—(Cornerstones of freedom)
    Includes index.
    Summary: An account of the first permanent English settlement in
North America, with all its tragedies and disasters, established in
1607 in Jamestown, Virginia.
    ISBN 0-516-20295-2 (lib.bdg.)   0-516-26138-X (pbk.)
    1. Jamestown (Va.)—History—Juvenile literature. 2. Virginia—
History—Colonial period, ca. 1600-1775—Juvenile literature.
[1. Jamestown (Va.)—History. 2. Virginia—History—Colonial period,
ca. 1600–1775.] I. Title. II. Series.
F234.J3S25   1997
975.5`4251—dc20
                                              96-24126
                                                 CIP
                                                  AC

On December 20, 1606, three small wooden ships set sail from England. Their names were *Susan Constant, Godspeed,* and *Discovery.* The ships carried 144 men and boys bound for North America. These travelers had one main goal—to establish the first permanent English colony in North America.

England claimed all the land in North America between Canada, which belonged to the French, and Florida, which was Spanish territory. The English called their entire territory Virginia.

Replicas of the Susan Constant, Godspeed, *and* Discovery *are docked at the Jamestown Settlement in Jamestown, Virginia.*

King James I

England had made two earlier attempts at colonization, but both failed. Then, in 1606, King James I of England granted colonization rights to the Virginia Company of London. The Virginia Company was a group of London merchants and wealthy gentlemen who supplied funds for the colony. In return, they expected to profit from the riches of North America. They were convinced that gold and silver were in Virginia, because the Spanish had already found these precious metals in South America.

The Virginia Company ordered the colonists to find gold and silver. The company also wanted the settlers to look for a water passageway to the Pacific Ocean. Such a shortcut would make it easier and more profitable to trade with Asia. The colonists were also supposed to convert the American Indians to Christianity.

The Virginia Company obtained three ships and hired Captain Christopher Newport to command them. Newport was in charge during the voyage; but a seven-man council, appointed by the Virginia Company, would take control once the colonists arrived in Virginia. The names of the council members would remain secret until landing.

After a four-month voyage, land was sighted at dawn on Sunday, April 26, 1607. The colonists had reached Virginia. That night, Captain Newport opened the sealed instructions from

The settlers sighted land on Sunday, April 26, 1607.

the Virginia Company and read aloud the names of the seven men who would lead the colony. The members of the governing council were Christopher Newport, Edward Wingfield, John Kendall, John Martin, John Ratcliffe, Bartholomew Gosnold, and John Smith.

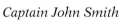

Captain John Smith

The colonists sailed across Chesapeake Bay and arrived at the mouth of a broad river. They named it the James River, in honor of their king. For two weeks, they explored both banks of the river, searching for a good location to settle.

The English settlers found American Indians throughout the area. These Indians were members of the Powhatan Confederacy, which was a group of more than thirty tribes ruled by the great Indian chief Powhatan. Nearly ten thousand Powhatan people lived in about two hundred villages spread across the rivers and shores of Chesapeake Bay. They lived in tunnel-shaped longhouses covered with tree bark. They hunted, fished, and raised corn, squash, and tobacco.

When the settlers arrived, they found American Indians of the Powhatan Confederacy living in the area.

Some American Indians were friendly. They welcomed the newcomers with feasts and dances. They traded corn and other food for beads and trinkets. But other Indians were not as friendly.

They shouted at the colonists and chased them away with a shower of arrows. They did not want these strangers settling on their land.

For their part, the settlers didn't respect the fact that the Indians had been living in Virginia for thousands of years. The British colonists believed that Virginia belonged to England, so they had a right to establish a colony there.

Late in the evening on May 13, 1607, the three wooden ships dropped anchor near a small peninsula of land in the James River. The settlers chose that location for their town because it would be easy to defend against attack from either land or sea. In addition, the water was deep enough for their ships to anchor close to the shore. They decided to call their settlement Jamestown.

The settlers honored King James I by naming their new home Jamestown.

The next morning, May 14, 1607, the settlers went ashore. First, the Reverend Robert Hunt held a church service. Then, the council members took a vote and elected Edward Wingfield as their president.

The colonists chopped down trees and began building a fort and a storehouse for their supplies. They cleared land and planted corn. One group of men cut clapboards. Another group searched for gold. Captain Newport took twenty-four men and explored upriver, looking unsuccessfully for a passage to the Pacific Ocean.

Colonist George Percy later wrote, "The fifteenth of June, we had built and finished our Fort." The triangular-shaped fort enclosed

By June 15, 1607, the settlers had built the fort where they lived.

The Jamestown fort was a triangular structure with cannons at each corner for protection against attacks.

nearly an acre of land. It measured 420 feet (128 meters) long on the river side and 300 feet (91 m) long on each of the other two sides. The main gate, located on the long side, faced the river and at each corner stood watchtowers with cannons mounted in them.

Along each inside wall of the fort was a row of houses with thatched roofs. The colonists also built a storehouse, a guardhouse, and a church inside the fort. Reverend Hunt held the first service in the new church on June 21, 1607.

The next day, June 22, Captain Newport left for England with a cargo of clapboards and a load of sparkling rocks that the colonists hoped were gold. Unfortunately, the rocks were only worthless iron pyrites, sometimes called "fool's gold." In time, the colonists realized that there was no gold at all in Virginia.

From the beginning, Jamestown was a poor location for a settlement. The area was low-lying marshland, and half of it was bogs and swamps that bred malaria-carrying mosquitoes. The narrow neck of the peninsula flooded at high tide, cutting the colony off from the mainland. There was no source of fresh drinking water. Water from the James River was salty at high tide and muddy at low tide.

Before long, the settlers became ill from drinking the unhealthy river water. They grew weak from lack of proper food. The colony was low on supplies, and the crops the men had planted were not yet ripe. They were unable to hunt, fish, or tend their fields because unfriendly American Indians lurked in the tall grass near the fort and shot arrows at anyone who ventured out. All through the summer people died,

More than half of the Jamestown settlers died by the end of their first summer in North America.

sometimes as many as three or four a day. By September, supplies were nearly gone and more than half the colonists were dead.

To make matters worse, the men in Jamestown often quarreled among themselves. Many of them were from England's upper class and were not used to working, so they did not have many practical skills.

Captain John Smith was an experienced soldier. He knew how to take care of himself and survive in the wilderness. Because of John Smith's abilities, the settlers turned to him for help. He was put in charge of trading beads and trinkets for corn and other food with the Indians. The food he obtained kept some of the remaining colonists from starving.

By trading with the Indians, John Smith (seated) obtained enough food to save some of the settlers from starvation.

In December 1607, while exploring the Chickahominy River, John Smith was captured by Powhatan Indians. The Indians took him to their leader, Chief Powhatan, at his village of Werowocomoco.

First, Powhatan gave Smith a huge feast. Then, the Indian chief ordered some men to bring in two large stones, which they placed at the chief's feet. Guards grabbed John Smith and forced his head down onto the stones. They raised their wooden clubs. Smith wrote that just as the guards were "ready with their clubs, to beat out [my] brains, Pocahontas the King's dearest daughter . . . got [my] head in her arms." Pocahontas was only about twelve years old when she saved John Smith's life.

Pocahontas begged her father, Powhatan (standing), to spare the life of John Smith.

Following this incident, Pocahontas visited Jamestown frequently, and she often served as a peacemaker between the English settlers and Powhatan's people. Once, she came to Jamestown to ask for the release of some Indians who had been taken prisoner. Captain Smith agreed to free the captives. Another time, she warned Smith that her people were planning to attack and kill him.

Pocahontas warned John Smith that her people were plotting to capture and murder him.

Captain Newport returned to Jamestown in January 1608 with 110 new colonists and badly needed supplies. A few days later, disaster struck. The fort and all but three of the buildings burned to the ground. The fire destroyed the church and the storehouse that contained most of the new supplies. The settlers had to rebuild the colony.

Throughout the winter of 1608, Pocahontas brought food to the hungry colonists. John Smith wrote, "Pocahontas was the instrument to preserve this colony from death, famine, and utter confusion."

Captain John Smith was elected president of Jamestown's council on September 10, 1608. Life in the colony began to improve under his leadership. He trained the men to fight. He made everyone work for their food. He sent groups of colonists up and down the river to live off the land as the Indians did.

John Smith explored and mapped Chesapeake Bay and its rivers. He drew a map of Virginia and wrote a history of Jamestown. Many English people became interested in coming to North America after they read his descriptions of Virginia.

At the end of September 1608, Captain Newport returned again with fresh supplies and seventy new settlers. Among them were the first women to arrive in Jamestown. Most of them

The first women arrived at Jamestown in September 1608.

were wives of the settlers who could finally join their husbands in the new colony.

Also in the autumn of 1608, the colonists set up a glass factory where they made bottles, drinking glasses, and windows. The factory was located on the mainland about a mile from the fort. The area became known as Glasshouse Point. The Jamestown glasshouse was the first factory in North America.

A re-creation of the Jamestown glasshouse

In 1609, John Smith suffered severe burns when his gunpowder bag accidentally caught on fire. His injuries were serious, and he went back to England for proper medical care. He never returned to Virginia. After Smith left, Pocahontas stopped coming to Jamestown, and the time of peace between the English and the Indians ended.

The Indians soon grew tired of the beads and trinkets that the colonists were trading. Instead,

Relations between the settlers and Indians grew steadily worse as minor disagreements grew into bitter confrontations.

they wanted guns and swords. When the English refused to give them weapons, the Indians started stealing them. When the Indians refused to trade for corn, the settlers took the corn by force. Sometimes the colonists burned the Indian villages and fields in revenge for Indian attacks on Jamestown. Over time, more colonists came to Virginia and their settlements spread out. Powhatan became increasingly angry about the English settlers taking more and more land. He continued to try to drive them away.

The winter of 1609–10 was the lowest point for the colony. Disease was widespread and many people were ill. Crops failed and the settlers ran out of food. The Indians continued to refuse to trade for corn. The colonists couldn't leave the fort to hunt or fish without being attacked by Indians. The colonists called that winter and the following spring the "Starving Time." Colonist George Percy wrote that starvation appeared ". . . in every face. . . . Of five hundred [people] we had only left about sixty, the rest being either starved through famine, or cut off by the [Indians]."

The settlers called the terrible winter of 1609–10 the "Starving Time."

By June 1610, the settlers decided to abandon the colony and return to England. On their way down the James River, they met the incoming ships of the new governor, Lord Delaware. He was arriving with supplies and 150 new settlers. The governor urged the colonists to turn around and return to Jamestown.

Governor Delaware imposed strict rules on the settlers and harsh penalties if the rules were broken. Stealing food and swearing were crimes punishable by death. Delaware put the settlers to work repairing the church and the fort. He sent men to build new settlements along the river. In 1611, 330 men went 60 miles (97 kilometers) up the James River to build a fort at a new town called Henrico.

Lord Delaware arrived with 150 new settlers in June 1610.

The colonists made several attempts to establish industries, but none were successful. As a result, Jamestown still depended on funds and supplies from England. The colony needed to find a source of income to become self-supporting.

One idea was to grow and sell tobacco because smoking was a popular pastime in Europe. But the native tobacco that grew wild in Virginia was too harsh and bitter for English tastes. In 1612, Jamestown settler John Rolfe obtained some tobacco seeds from the Caribbean islands. He also began experimenting with new methods of growing and harvesting that produced a sweet, mild tobacco. The Virginia soil and climate proved to be perfect for tobacco cultivation.

The colonists worked hard to develop a tobacco industry.

In 1613, the first shipment of the new tobacco left Virginia for England. Two years later, the colony exported 2,300 pounds (1,043 kilograms) of tobacco. By 1616, tobacco was the main crop of the colony. Every family grew some tobacco alongside their vegetables and hung the tobacco leaves indoors to dry.

In 1617, the Virginia colony exported 20,000 pounds (9,072 kg) of tobacco. Just two years later tobacco export jumped to 45,000 pounds (20,411 kg). The rich golden leaves of the tobacco plant finally made the colony self-supporting.

In 1613, the same year that the first tobacco shipment left Virginia, Pocahontas returned to Jamestown by force. She had been visiting friends in the Potomac region when Captain Samuel Argall arrived there on a trading mission. Argall saw an opportunity to force Powhatan into a peace treaty. He tricked Pocahontas into coming aboard his ship, then sailed with her to Jamestown. Argall planned to hold Pocahontas hostage until Powhatan

Captain Samuel Argall kidnapped Pocahontas and planned to hold her for ransom until Powhatan met his demands.

released English prisoners captured by the Indians, returned stolen weapons, and agreed to make peace with the colonists. It took three months for Powhatan to reply to Argall's demands.

Meanwhile, Jamestown's governor, Thomas Gates, had sent Pocahontas to stay at Henrico. There, Pocahontas learned to speak English. She was also taught the manners of a "proper" Englishwoman. The Reverend Alexander Whitaker taught her about Christian beliefs. Eventually, Pocahontas decided to become a Christian. She was baptized and took a new name, Rebecca.

Pocahontas was taught to dress and speak like an Englishwoman.

Pocahontas (kneeling) was baptized at Henrico and took the name Rebecca.

John Rolfe and Pocahontas were married on April 5, 1614.

While she was living at Henrico, Pocahontas met the tobacco planter, John Rolfe. Soon, the two fell in love. They asked Jamestown's governor and Powhatan for permission to marry. The governor and the Indian chief both agreed to the marriage.

Pocahontas married John Rolfe on April 5, 1614, in the little church at Jamestown. The following year, their son, Thomas, was born. Their marriage ended the fighting between the settlers and the American Indians. The peace, which lasted eight years, was called the "Peace of Pocahontas."

Although conditions had improved at Jamestown, investors in England grew tired of the colony's many problems. They turned their attention—and their money—to Bermuda, England's newest colony. The Virginia Company had to win back the investors because it needed their money to send more people and supplies to Virginia.

In 1616, the Virginia Company decided to send the Rolfe family to England on a goodwill visit. The people of England were fascinated by Pocahontas; but she was not used to the damp, chilly English weather and the polluted air of London. She became very ill. On the day Pocahontas was supposed to return to America, she died. She was buried at St. George's Parish Church in Gravesend, England, on March 21, 1617.

John Rolfe went back to Virginia, but Thomas remained with relatives in England. He returned to North America when he was about twenty years old and became a prosperous Virginia planter.

The gravesite of Pocahontas at St. George's Parish Church in Gravesend, England

The year 1619 brought many changes to Jamestown. The first representative legislature in North America met in the Jamestown church on July 30. The Virginia Company created the House of Burgesses to satisfy the colonists' demands for a greater voice in their government. Two burgesses were elected in each of the colony's eleven settlements. Together, the House of Burgesses, the governor, and his council formed the General Assembly of Virginia. The Assembly met once a year to make laws for the Virginia colony. All the current state and national legislatures in the United States are descended from this first Assembly.

In August, a Dutch ship brought the first Africans to Virginia. They were sold at auction as indentured servants. Many English people also came to North America as indentured servants. Under this system, a servant agreed

The first Africans were brought to North America as indentured servants.

to work for a master for a certain length of time, usually four to seven years. In return, the servant received passage from England, and food, clothing, and shelter during the period of service. Servants sometimes received supplies and land at the end of their service to equip them for their new lives as free men and women.

As the colony expanded and the tobacco industry grew, the need for cheap labor grew as well. With this demand, slavery increased in popularity. African slaves eventually replaced indentured servants as the main source of cheap labor.

Auctions encouraged the replacement of indentured servitude with slavery.

Between 1619 and 1621, forty-two ships carried 3,570 new settlers to Virginia. The colony continued to expand and squeeze the American Indians out of their territory. Chief Opechancanough had become the leader of the Powhatan Indians after Powhatan's death in 1618. He decided to get rid of the English once and for all. On March 22, 1622, Opechancanough led an Indian massacre that killed 347 colonists.

In December of that year, the English ship *Abigail* arrived with new settlers. Unfortunately, most of the passengers were ill with a contagious disease. The disease spread quickly through the colony, and hundreds of people died. By the end of 1622, only about five hundred people were left in the entire colony of Virginia.

In spite of massacres, diseases, fires, and other disasters, settlers continued to flock to Virginia. By 1625, there were 1,232 people living in 25 locations in Virginia, including 124 people in Jamestown.

As time passed, Jamestown and all of Virginia grew and prospered. Then, on April 18, 1644, Opechancanough's people attacked the

In 1622, chief Opechancanough led the Indians in an attack that killed 347 colonists.

colonists again. This second massacre killed more than five hundred settlers. But by this time the colony was much stronger, and the Indian uprising was crushed.

In 1676, Nathaniel Bacon led a group of planters in a revolt against Governor William Berkeley. The planters demanded better protection against Indian raids and greater participation in the colony's government. The rebels captured Jamestown, but when they realized that they could not hold the town indefinitely, they burned it to the ground. When Bacon died suddenly of malaria on October 26, 1676, the revolt collapsed.

Nathaniel Bacon (center) and a group of supporters led a revolt against Governor William Berkeley (left) in 1676.

Jamestown was rebuilt, but it never completely recovered from the chaos of the rebellion. On October 21, 1698, the statehouse in Jamestown burned again, this time accidentally. As a result of the fire, the burgesses decided to move the capital 8 miles (13 km) inland to the town of Middle Plantation. The following year, Middle Plantation was renamed Williamsburg in honor of the British king, William III. It became the capital of Virginia, and Jamestown fell into decay.

Over the years, erosion changed the banks of the James River and washed away much of the original peninsula. The neck of land joining the peninsula to the mainland disappeared under the river's currents, turning Jamestown into an island. For many years, historians thought that the location of the original fort lay underwater.

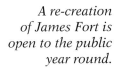

A re-creation of James Fort is open to the public year round.

But in 1996, archeologists uncovered what they believe are artifacts from the first settlement and evidence of the 1607 fort. Continuing research will increase knowledge about the Jamestown Colony.

Today, Jamestown Island is part of the Colonial National Historical Park. The island is jointly owned and managed by the United States National Park Service and the Association for the Preservation of Virginia Antiquities.

More than a million people visit the Jamestown area each year to experience what life was like during the early days of the first permanent English colony in North America. Although the Jamestown colony itself no longer exists, its legacy lives on.

Foundations of settlers' buildings are part of Colonial National Historical Park in Jamestown, Virginia.

GLOSSARY

burgess – citizen elected to represent a settlement or district

capital – location of the government of a colony, state, or country

clapboard – long, narrow board used to cover the outer walls of buildings

colony – new territory that is settled by people who are governed by another country

council – group of people elected or appointed to serve as advisors or leaders

cultivation – the growing of crops

erosion – the slow wearing or washing away of the earth's surface

famine

famine – great lack of food

legislature – group of people responsible for making laws for a colony, state, or country

longhouse – American-Indian home built of poles and bark

malaria – disease caused by infected mosquitoes that produces fever, chills, sweating, and sometimes, death

natural resource – useful material found in nature such as wood, fresh water, or minerals

peninsula – body of land surrounded by water on three sides

thatch

thatch – reeds, straw, or thick grasses used to cover the roof of a building

TIMELINE

	1607	*May 14:* Jamestown Colony founded, Pocahontas saves John Smith
First women arrive, glass factory built	**1608**	
	1609	} "Starving Time"
	1610	
	1613	
	1614	*April 5:* Pocahontas marries John Rolfe
	1617	*March 21:* Pocahontas dies in England
	1619	
	1620	Plymouth Colony founded (Massachusetts)
	1622	*March 22:* First Indian attack
	1644	*April 18:* Second Indian attack
	1676	
Capital moves to Williamsburg	**1699**	
American War of Independence {	**1775**	
	1776	*July 4:* Declaration of Independence signed
	1781	

First tobacco shipment leaves Jamestown, Pocahontas kidnapped

July 30: First legislative assembly meets

September: First Africans arrive

Bacon's Rebellion

DEDICATION
For Matoaka

INDEX *(Boldface page numbers indicate illustrations.)*

PHOTO CREDITS
©: Cameramann International Ltd.: 2; Colonial National Historical Park: 5 top, 6, 8, 10, 11, 16, 18, 19, 27, 31 bottom right, 31 top left; Colonial Williamsburg Foundation: 4, 9; Corbis-Bettmann: 17, 21 top, 30 top; Dave G. Houser: 15 bottom, 28, 30 bottom; H. Armstrong Roberts: 1 (R. Krubner), 3 (D. Campione); James P. Rowan: 29; Jamestown-Yorktown Educational Trust: cover, 13, 20, 22, 26; North Wind Picture Archives: 5 bottom, 12, 15 top, 25; Photri: 23; Stock Montage, Inc.: 21 bottom, 24, 31 center; Superstock, Inc.: 7.

ABOUT THE AUTHOR
Gail Sakurai is a children's author who specializes in retelling folktales and writing nonfiction for young readers. She is a member of the Society of Children's Book Writers and Illustrators. *The Jamestown Colony* is her fifth book. Other books she has written for Children's Press include *Stephen Hawking: Understanding the Universe, Mae Jemison: Space Scientist,* and *The Liberty Bell.*

Ms. Sakurai lives in Cincinnati, Ohio, with her husband and two sons. When she is not researching or writing, she enjoys traveling with her family and visiting America's historical sites.